40 PRAYERS

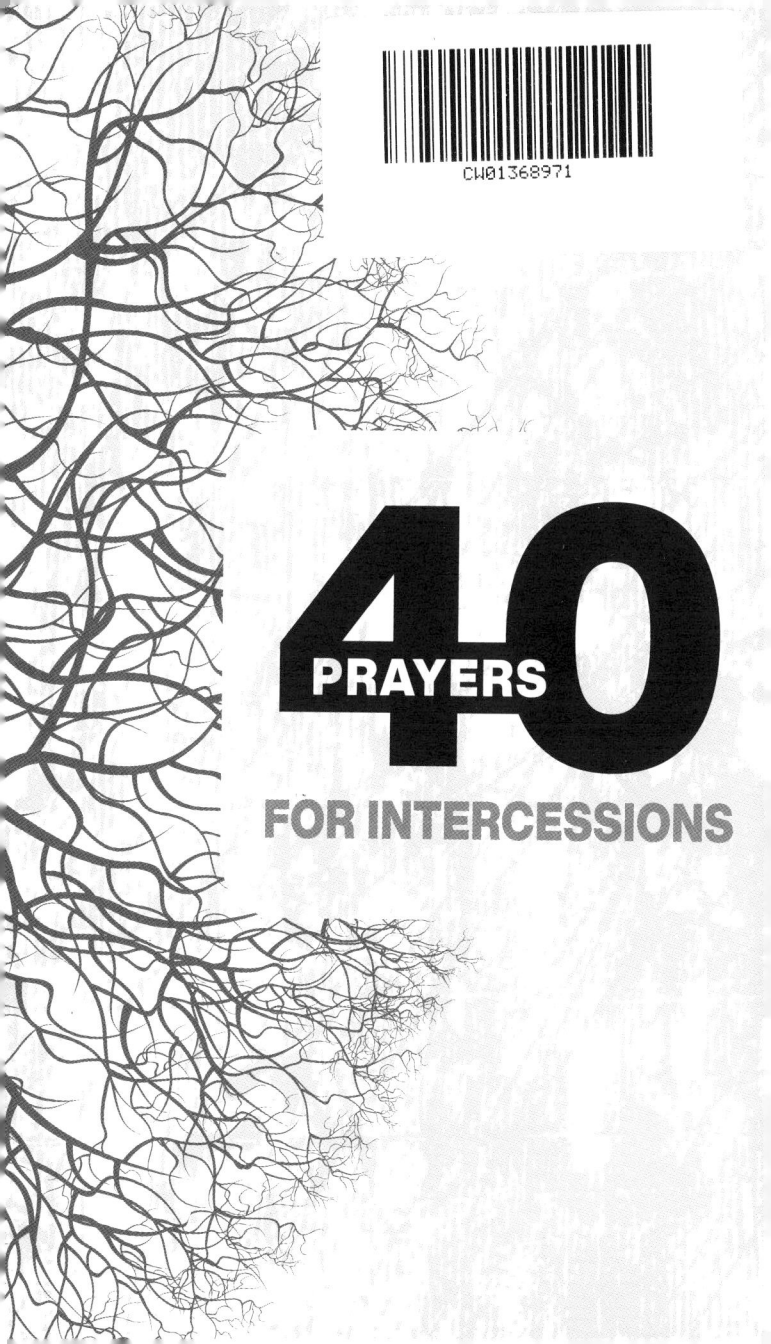

FOR INTERCESSIONS

40 PRAYERS FOR INTERCESSIONS

Prayers for your Church or small group

DAVID CLOWES

transforming lives together

40 PRAYERS FOR INTERCESSIONS
Published by David C Cook
4050 Lee Vance Drive
Colorado Springs, CO 80918 U.S.A.

Integrity Music Limited, a Division of David C Cook
Brighton, East Sussex BN1 2RE, England

The graphic circle C logo is a registered trademark of David C Cook.

All rights reserved. Except for brief excerpts for review purposes, no part of this book may be reproduced or used in any form without written permission from the publisher.

The website addresses recommended throughout this book are offered as a resource to you. These websites are not intended in any way to be or imply an endorsement on the part of David C Cook, nor do we vouch for their content.

ISBN 978-0-8307-8237-6
eISBN 978-0-8307-8245-1

© 2021 David Clowes

The Team: Ian Matthews, Jack Campbell,
Jo Stockdale, Susan Murdock
Cover Design: Pete Barnsley

Printed in the United Kingdom
First Edition 2021

1 2 3 4 5 6 7 8 9 10

INTRODUCTION

Having published *500 Prayers for All Occasions* and *500 More Prayers for All Occasions* I was asked to develop a new series of books of prayer for use in small groups or in the home.

There are at least forty prayers in each of these books based around a single theme. Most of the content comes from my first two books of prayer for public worship, but has been revised and re-worked to make it appropriate for use in churches, small groups, the family situation, or for personal quiet time devotions.

My church background was firmly in the camp of extemporary prayer. I started to write my prayers down due to nervousness and on the advice of my preaching mentor who insisted on careful preparation not only of the hymns, readings, and sermon, but also of the prayers. I have long since realised the value of having a resource to be used as a flexible launch pad for my own prayer life which I could use and adapt as I wished.

I hope that is how you will approach these simple aids to prayer. They have been deliberately written in an uncomplicated style and with language that seeks to illuminate the joy of prayer. I have also tried to ensure that they are written in the language we use in our daily conversations. The aim of this is designed to make them easier to 'pray' and not simply to 'read'.

David Clowes
Stockport, April 2020

ONE WORLD

Lord, we pray for those who are
 hungry in a world of plenty;
for those who do not know
 where their next meal
 is coming from;
and for those who can only
 watch as their children die.
Lord, help us to provide
 for them.
The Lord hears our prayer.
Thanks be to God.

Lord, we pray for those who
 cry for justice for the poor;
for those who speak out
 for those whose voices
 are not heard;
and for those who work
 unselfishly for those who
 cannot work for themselves.
Lord, give them strength
 in their endeavours.
The Lord hears our prayer.
Thanks be to God.

Lord, we pray for those who
 do not want our pity—
they simply want a new chance;
for those who do not
 want our help—
they simply want fairness;
for those who need aid,
 but would rather
be allowed the opportunity
 to live and to grow
 for themselves.
Please open up new
 opportunities for them.
The Lord hears our prayer.
Thanks be to God.

Lord, we pray for the
 church, your people
 throughout the world.
We ask for the courage to speak
 for those deprived of a voice;
the willingness to share
 the pain of those whose
 hands are empty;
and the power to stand up for
 the powerless, the lost, and
those with no hope—and
 to go on standing, no
 matter the cost.
The Lord hears our prayer.
Thanks be to God.

In the name of Christ, who
    like the Father is always on
    the side of the poor. **Amen.**

THOSE WHO REMEMBER

*Prepare a set of four candles.
Light a new candle as you
begin each prayer.*

We light this candle for
    those who remember
the ones who went to war
    and never returned;
who set out in the prime of life
and whose bodies and minds
    and lives were damaged
by all they had seen and heard.
May the light of Christ bring
    peace to the world.

silence

We light this candle for
    those who remember
the high hopes and exciting
    dreams that once were theirs;
for those whose lives
    have been wrecked
by addictions that now
    rule their lives;
and for those who are left to
    ponder their 'if onlys' and
    their 'might have beens'.
May the light of Christ bring
    peace to their hearts.

silence

We light this candle for
    those who seem unable
    to remember
people and places that
    once meant so much;
for those who sit alone with
    no one to visit them,
no one to brighten their day;
and for those whose memories
    are all that they have left
but who have no one to
    share them with.
May the light of Christ
    heal broken hearts.

silence

We light this candle for
    anyone we know to be
    in need of our prayers;
for those whose lives have
    been devastated
by disaster or disease, by
    depression or despair.

silence

Lord, in your mercy,
hear our prayer. Amen.

COME AS THE LIGHT

Lord, we pray for those
    whose lives are trapped
    by the darkness of fear;
for those facing a time of
    uncertainty, illness,

and the fear that comes
   from not knowing;
for those in hospital,
   and those undergoing
   unpleasant treatment;
for those who wait through
   dark days of anxiety.
Lord, in the darkness,
come as the light.

Lord, we pray for those in the
   darkness of loneliness;
for those who are single in a
   society designed for the family
and for those left alone now
   the family have gone;
for those who spend their days
   in the prison of their home
and long for someone to visit,
   to break into the silence
   of their aloneness;
for those who with the passing
   years have only their memories
and no one with whom
   to share them.
Lord, in the darkness,
come as the light.

Lord, we pray for those in the
   darkness of emptiness;
for those who have filled their
   days and their hours
with the passing pleasures
   of the moment
and are discovering that
   the security, peace, and
   contentment they promised
were but a mirage that could
   never last in the reality
   of the coming day;
for those whose riches account
   for nothing of value;
and for those whose
   hollowness is bringing
   them pain and despair.
Lord, in the darkness,
come as the light.

Lord, we pray for those
   whose lives have been
   darkened by disaster;
for those whose lives have
   been destroyed
by the impact of earthquake,
   flood, or fire;
for those who have lost
   everything and everyone
   that mattered to them
and for those facing hunger
   and starvation through
   no fault of their own;
for those struggling
   for existence
and for those who know that
   they are losing the fight.
Lord, in the darkness,
come as the light.

Lord, we pray for those
   we know by name,
that the light of Christ will
   bring them the joy of
   renewal and refreshment.

We pray too for ourselves,
   that the light of Christ
   will find its way
even into the darkest
   corners of our lives,
that we might walk in
   the light of his love.
Lord, in the darkness,
come as the light.

We bring our prayers in the
   name of Christ, the Light
   of the world. **Amen.**

PETER AND CORNELIUS

Lord, we pray for those who
   listen to the voice of the poor;
for those who speak out
   on behalf of those
with no hope, no meaning,
   and no future;
for those with the power
   to change things
and for those who are calling
   us to act before it's too late.
May they share with us all
   their vision of compassion.
Lord of life and time
   and eternity,
listen to our prayer.

Lord, we pray for those who
   listen to the cry for justice;
for those imprisoned for
   their political ideals or
   their faith in Christ;
for those who work tirelessly
for people locked up without
   trial and for crimes they
   did not commit.
May they share with others
   their vision of truth.
Lord of life and time
   and eternity,
listen to our prayer.

Lord, we pray for those who
   listen to the silent suffering
of the hungry and starving,
   especially [*name a
   recent tragedy*],
who seek to cross boundaries
   and reach out today
on behalf of those who may
   have no tomorrow.
May they challenge us all
   with their vision of hope.
Lord of life and time
   and eternity,
listen to our prayer.

Lord, we pray for those who
   listen to you speaking
through the ones whom
   they meet;
for those who hear you calling
   through what they can see;
for those who, like Peter
   and Cornelius, allow
   you to speak to them
in the most unexpected of ways
and go on listening at
   times and in places,

even when they feel
 unprepared to respond.
May their vision of expectancy
 encourage us all.
Lord of life and time
 and eternity,
listen to our prayer.

In the name of the Lord of life
 and time and eternity. **Amen.**

THOSE ON THE OUTSIDE

Lord, we pray for those who feel
that they are on the outside
 of life just looking in;
those with no home, no
 food, and no future;
those with no hope, no
 joy, and no love;
those with no courage, no
 strength, and no purpose;
those with no laughter,
 no joy, and no one to
 share their tears.

We pray for those who long
 to be held but have no
 one to hold them;
those who have hopes
 and dreams but no
 one to share them;
those who are weary,
 weighed down with worry
 and responsibility,
but have no one to
 walk with them.

We pray for those who are
 so busy 'doing' that they
 have no time just to 'be';
those who have forgotten to pray
and have yet to discover that
 you are still listening;
those to whom you
 are a stranger,
who still need to learn that
 their names and their days
 are precious to you.
May they yet discover
 that in Christ
all things hold together
 and all things can be
 made new. **Amen.**

BROKEN IMAGES

We pray for those with
 fragile images;
those whose picture of life has
 been centred on themselves;
those who have sought to
 find fulfilment, purpose,
 and satisfaction
in the accumulation of
 material possessions
and those who place great
 importance on how others
 think about them.
May they find in Christ a
 picture of renewal and hope
when their images of life
 have been broken.
Lord of life,
this is our prayer.

We pray for those with
  damaged images;
those whose journey had
  been untroubled, peaceful,
  and undisturbed,
for whom good health was
  taken for granted,
success was always assured,
  and life held no fears
  or disappointments;
for those who are now
  facing times of trial,
  uncertainty, and pain.
May they find in Christ a
  picture of renewal and hope
when their images of life
  have been broken.
Lord of life,
this is our prayer.

We pray for those whose
  image of life is too shallow
and who settle too easily
  for too little, too soon;
for those whose vision of
  life is extremely limited
and whose plans, hopes,
  and expectations
are focused on their own
  wants, needs, and dreams;
for those whose image of
  life is all pleasure
and is centred on the
  excitement that
  today can bring.
May they find in Christ a
  picture of renewal and hope
when their images of life
  have been broken.
Lord of life,
this is our prayer.

We pray for those whose
  image of life stops short of
  their neighbour's door;
for those whose short-
  sightedness enables them
to ignore the suffering of others
and whose deafness
  prevents them hearing
  the cries of the poor;
for those who turn a blind eye
  to the deprivation of others
and for those who pretend
  they are unaware
of the injustice their brothers
  and sisters are facing.
May they find in Christ a
  picture of renewal and hope
when their images of life
  have been broken.
Lord of life,
this is our prayer.

We bring all our prayers
  in the name of him
who offered bread and
  wine as the image of his
  love for us all. **Amen.**

THOSE WHO ARE ANXIOUS

Lord, we pray for those who
  are anxious about the past;

for those who are troubled today
by memories of their yesterdays
   that won't go away;
for those whose memories
   still cause them to grieve
and remain a barrier to freedom,
   peace, and contentment.
The Lord is our strength
   and our song,
and he will hold us for ever.

Lord, we pray for those who are
   anxious about tomorrow;
for those whose whole lives
   are crippled by the fear
of what the future might hold;
for those who can find no peace,
   no comfort, and no joy
because they are overwhelmed
   by a sense of doubt
   and uncertainty;
for those whose fear of failure
   limits their horizons
and for those whose dread
   robs each new day
of the sense of fulfilment that
   could have been theirs.
The Lord is our strength
   and our song,
and he will hold us for ever.

Lord, we pray for those who
   are anxious about today;
for those who know what
   today will bring;
for those who are sinking
   under the weight
of the responsibilities
   heaped upon them
and who see no way to
   lighten their load;
for those for whom each
   day is filled with a
   sense of foreboding
and for those who are
   slowly being wrung dry
   by their concerns
for their family, their
   neighbour, and the world
   of pain and despair.
The Lord is our strength
   and our song,
and he will hold us for ever.

Lord, we pray for those who
   are simply anxious
and can give no reason for
   their anxiety within;
for those whose anxiety
   robs them of sleep
and daily leaves them
   seeking in vain
for an experience of
   rest and renewal;
for those who feel foolish
   for being so anxious
and count themselves failures
   when they are not to blame;
for those who live out their
   lives under a cloud of
   defeat and depression;
for those driven to the
   limits of coping

and for those whose greatest
    need is just to be loved.
The Lord is our strength
    and our song,
and he will hold us for ever.

Lord, we pray for those who
    are anxious for others
and for those whose concern for
    family, friends, and neighbours
outstrips their capacity
    to respond;
for those who carry the
    burdens of the world
    on their shoulders
and for those whose joy, hope,
    and peace are destroyed
by anguish for the plight of
    the hungry and starving
and the endless stream
    of refugees implanted
    in their minds by the
    work of the media.
The Lord is our strength
    and our song,
and he will hold us for ever.

In the name of Christ, who
    holds us all, for ever. **Amen.**

TRUST

We pray for those who have
    put their trust in you
and have found that it has
    brought them pain, rejection,
    and a sense of isolation.

We pray for those who, because
    of their faith in Christ,
have lost their home, their
    freedom, and their
    family and friends;
for those who face persecution
    because of their stand
    for the truth.
May the love of Christ sustain
    their hope and their faith.
The Lord hears our prayer.
Thanks be to God.

We pray for those in
    positions of leadership;
for Christians who are
    Members of Parliament
and find great anguish in the
    choices that they must make;
for those who are tempted
    to sacrifice their principles
    for the sake of personal
    power and status
and for those who are still
    genuinely seeking equal
    opportunity for all.
The Lord hears our prayer.
Thanks be to God.

We pray for the life of
    all churches and for
    all their members
and for those who are in danger
    of losing sight of Christ
    and of their hold on him;
for those for whom
    worship has become an
    empty weekly ritual

and fellowship with other
   Christians a distant memory;
for those who no longer
   read their Bible
and for whom prayer
   is a hurried jumble
   of vague words.
May the love of Christ
   revive his church, and
   may it begin with me.
The Lord hears our prayer.
Thanks be to God.

We pray for those who are
   enemies of all that is
   good, true, and right;
for those whose words
   lead others astray
and for those whose example
   causes pain to many;
for those whose abuse of
   their power has hurt
   their neighbours
and for those whose abuse of
   other people's lives and bodies
has left scars that are
   slow to heal.
We pray for those responsible
   for what appears in
   the printed media
and for what we see on
   our televisions.
May the love of Christ
   transform their
   hearts and lives.
The Lord hears our prayer.
Thanks be to God.

We ask all our prayers
   in the name of Christ
   our Lord. **Amen.**

I AM ...

I am just a child—well,
   I am inside.
What happened to me all those
   years ago has left its scars.
Today it's called abuse—then
   it was just 'our little secret'.
And so I bottled everything
   up inside—
all the hurt, the pain,
   and the shame.
I know, deep down, it
   wasn't my fault
but it has still made it very
   hard for me to trust
   anyone, ever again.
It is as if I am a coiled
   spring—I'm all screwed up
and I hide myself away
   from your gaze.
You have no idea just how
   much I long to be free,
to be the 'me' I know
   God intended.
Pray for me.

silence

I am a person who is ill.
The problem for me is that
   I don't really know what's
   the matter with me.

Nobody tells me, and that
   makes me very upset.
They stand at the end of
   my bed and they speak
   in hushed tones.
They think I can't hear
but every word they speak
   hammers fear and doubt
   into my brain.
I lie there and think
   about life—my life.
Could I have done
   things differently?
Could I have cared more?
Could I have been more
   understanding?
Could I have made more
   time for God?
I don't know what time I have
   left—but I just want to live.
Pray for me.

silence

I am a social worker.
I hate to admit it because
   to many people it's
   like a rude word.
But to me it was a calling:
I believed God wanted
   me to serve him in this
   way—I still do.
Whether my clients are old
   or young, I always try to
   do my best for them.
Yes, sometimes I do get
   things wrong.

It's because I'm human
   that I make mistakes.
When something goes wrong
   I give myself a hard time
and I can do without the media
   hitting me when I'm down.
You have no idea how
   much it would help
if someone, somewhere, stopped
   and said thank you.
Pray for me.

silence

I am a church member.
I have attended church
   all my life;
I can't remember a day or a time
   when I didn't believe in God.
I have held every office
   in the church
and I have said my prayers
   and read my Bible
for as long as I can remember.
I envy those who speak
   of their personal
   relationship with Jesus
and who can worship with such
   a sense of the presence of God.
Deep down, I know, I only
   wish it could happen to me.
Pray for me.

silence

Lord, in your mercy,
hear our prayer. Amen.

THE MIND OF CHRIST

We pray for those whose
  minds are filled with anger;
for those whose lives
  are wrecked by the
  bitterness within them
and for those who feel
  that they have been
  betrayed by society,
that it did not protect them
  from the evil of other people.
May the mind of Christ
  soften their hard hearts.
This is our prayer.
We ask it in Christ's name.

We pray for those whose
  minds are filled with
  uncertainty and fear;
for those whose homes
  have suffered the
  effects of burglary
and for those whose peace
  and sense of security
  it has destroyed;
for those whose minds
  are in turmoil
and for those overwhelmed
  by their sense of
  responsibility for others;
for those who give themselves
  no peace, no space, and
  no freedom just to be.
May the mind of Christ fill
  them with his peace.
This is our prayer.
We ask it in Christ's name.

We pray for those who struggle
  with the onset of dementia;
for those who are finding
  it hard to understand
  who they are
and for those whose memories
  seem to have been lost;
for those who can no longer
  share the memories
  they still have
and for those who are grieving
  for the person that they
  used to know and love.
May the mind of Christ
  give them hope.
This is our prayer.
We ask it in Christ's name.

We pray for those whose
  minds are focused on
  the daily search for the
  needs of the body;
for those who are hungry
  and starving
and for those in desperate
  need for the medicines
  we take for granted;
for those whose thoughts are
  affected by their poverty
and by the appalling conditions
  in which they exist;
for politicians who turn
  a blind eye to the real
  needs of their people
and for those who genuinely
  care but are overwhelmed
  by the scale of the task.

40 PRAYERS FOR INTERCESSIONS

May the mind of Christ bring
them courage and hope.
This is our prayer.
We ask it in Christ's name.

We pray for ourselves and the
thoughts that fill our minds;
for our concerns for those
who are ill, in hospital
and for those whose pain and
sorrow touch our hearts;
for those whose fears,
worries, and anguish allow
us no rest or peace,
and for our need to be open
to God and to value
ourselves just as he does.
May the mind of Christ bring
us contentment and life.
This is our prayer.
**We ask it in Christ's
name. Amen.**

DELIVERANCE

Lord, we pray for those enslaved
by their love of money
and ensnared by their grasping
after material possessions;
for those who worship
wealth and status
and are for ever searching
for fulfilment
in their false hope in the
pot of gold at the end
of their rainbow.
Lord, do not bring us to
the time of trial,
but deliver us from evil.

Lord, we pray for those
whose lives are trapped in
their commitment to
the false gods of self-
aggrandisement,
self-centredness, and
self-satisfaction;
for those who have lost
their way in the labyrinth
of New Age worship
and the idolisation of
'mother earth'
with no awareness of
their dependence on
their creator God.
Lord, do not bring us to
the time of trial,
but deliver us from evil.

Lord, we pray for those trapped
by their web of lies
and whose whole way of life
is stained by their greed,
pride, and self-interest;
for those whose lifestyle is built
on the sandy foundations of
corruption and falsehood
and for those whose attitudes
and values are a danger to
the weak and the vulnerable.
Lord, do not bring us to
the time of trial,
but deliver us from evil.

Lord, we pray for those caught
    by the lure of illegal drugs
and the instant solution
    they seem to offer to
    their problems;
for those too afraid to
    say no, to stand out,
    or to be different;
for those who are finding
    that their bodies are
    still being damaged
even by drugs labelled
    'recreational';
for those who turn to crime
    to fund their habit
and for those who are
    craving deliverance.
Lord, do not bring us to
    the time of trial,
but deliver us from evil.

Lord, we pray for those
    who plant bombs
and who give no thought
    to the suffering and
    death they create;
for terrorists who see only
    the cause to which
    they are committed
and refuse to see the cost
    that others bear through
    no fault of their own;
for those whose unsocial
    behaviour destroys
    communities
and robs their neighbours of
    the peace they long for.

Lord, do not bring us to
    the time of trial,
but deliver us from evil.

Lord, we bring our prayers
    for freedom from all
    that spoils our lives
in the name of Christ the
    deliverer. **Amen.**

THE COMMUNITY

Heavenly Father, we pray
    for those who are called
    to serve in the world;
for all leaders of nations,
    politicians, company
    directors, newspaper editors,
    and television producers;
for those who work for
    Christian Aid, Tearfund,
    CAFOD, Save the Children,
and for every Christian
    who travels anywhere
    in the world,
that they may be
    ambassadors for Christ.
This is our prayer.
We ask it in Jesus' name.

Heavenly Father, we pray for
    those who are called to serve
    in the local community;
for doctors, nurses, and
    all who work in the
    National Health Service

and for teachers, police officers,
 probation officers, care
 workers, and social workers;
for shopkeepers, secretaries,
 and those who keep
 our streets clean
and for firemen, factory workers,
 and all who provide the power
 and water for our homes;
for parents, neighbours,
 and friends.
May they know that in serving
 others they are serving you.
This is our prayer.
We ask it in Jesus' name.

Heavenly Father, we pray for all
 who are called to serve you
 in and through your church;
for all ministers, lay preachers,
 Sunday school teachers,
 and house group leaders
and for our church officers,
 door stewards, and
 pastoral visitors;
for those who serve as treasurers,
 members of committees,
 and church councils;
for all who are called to
 serve in the background
 preparing refreshments,
cleaning, or repairing the
 premises and for those
 who support mission
 at home or overseas.
This is our prayer.
We ask it in Jesus' name.

Heavenly Father, we
 pray for ourselves.
We remember that you have
 called us to serve you
 here and everywhere.
You call us to serve where we
 are today and where you
 will lead us in the future.
You call us to serve you
 with the time, skills, and
 gifts we have now
and with those we shall
 receive in days to come.
Help us to remember our task
 is bringing glory, praise,
 and honour to your name
wherever in the world
 you send us
that we may be enabled
 to serve you in the way
 that you choose.
This is our prayer.
**We ask it in Jesus'
 name. Amen.**

THE HUNGRY

Lord, we pray for those who
 are hungry for food;
for those who today will
 have nothing to eat
and for those who will go
 to sleep not knowing if
 they will eat tomorrow;
for those whose gaunt, empty
 faces rebuke our greed,
 our self-satisfaction,

and challenge our
   easy acceptance of
   injustice for others
and our wealth that comes to us
   at the expense of their hope.
Lord of the poor,
hear our prayer.

Lord, we pray for those who
   are hungry for love;
for those who have never
   known what it means to
   be loved unconditionally
and for those who have felt
   unwanted, unnecessary,
   and unloved
for as long as they can
   remember;
for those who have lost
   people they loved and
   people who loved them;
for those whose lives are
   crippled by their sense of
   rejection and desertion
and for those whose vision
   of life is coloured by
   memories that hurt
and a future that is now seen
   through a veil of tears.
Lord of the poor,
hear our prayer.

Lord, we pray for those who
   are hungry for justice;
for those who work long
   hours for pay that is little
   more than a pittance
and for those with no voice of
   their own to rescue them
from life-destroying and
   dangerous work;
for those forced to
   live in squalor
and whose bodies and skills
   are exploited by others;
for those who sit and stare
because they have no way
   to satisfy their hunger for
   freedom and justice.
Lord of the poor,
hear our prayer.

Lord, we pray for those who
   are hungry for peace;
for those who have witnessed
   the appalling impact of war
and for those scarred by
   the horrors of violence
   and civil unrest;
for those whose lives are
   in turmoil and whose
   aching and loneliness
is hidden from the eyes of
   the world but is seen by
   the heart of the Father;
for those whose every
   waking moment is
   touched by memories
of the wrong choices and
   the foolish decisions
   they have made.
Lord of the poor,
hear our prayer.

We pray for ourselves and
   all the things we hunger
   to know and to be;
for those memories we long to
   forget and the forgiveness
   we know we must give;
for the hunger inside that
   nothing in this world
   can ever satisfy
and for the promise of
   cleansing, renewal, and
   fulfilment as we receive
   the Spirit of Christ.
Lord of the poor,
hear our prayer.

All this we pray for Jesus
   Christ's sake. **Amen.**

THE WORLD, THE NATION, THE CHURCH, AND THE COMMUNITY

Lord, we pray for the world,
   your world, that you made
   to bring you glory,
to reflect your creative love, and
   to be a place where everyone
   could find fulfilment in you.
But we have changed your
   law of love for the demand
   of first come, first served,
the law of the jungle, a world
   where might is right,
and where gentleness,
   mercy, and compassion
   are in short supply.
Lord, in your mercy,
hear our prayer.

We pray for our nation
   which once was known as
   a Christian country and
   for its Christian values.
We used to be a society
   that based our law and
   our life on your Word
and where we knew what was
   right and what was wrong.
We pray for our nation,
   where everyone does what
   is right in their own eyes
and no longer is there a special
   day for the worship of God
and a time for spiritual
   refreshment for all.
Lord, in your mercy,
hear our prayer.

We pray for our community
   where people once cared
   for one another
and where neighbours gave
   support to those in need,
for our community
   where people once
   felt safe and secure
and where people were content
   with simple pleasures
and knew the difference
   between needs and wants;
for our community where
   people suffer in isolation
   and die all alone

and where people are
   afraid to help others
   because compassion
has been replaced by self-
   centred concern.
Lord, in your mercy,
hear our prayer.

We pray for people who feel
   lost, defeated, and lonely;
for those who look back
   to 'might have beens'
   and to 'if onlys'
and for those afraid of what
   the future may bring;
for those who have filled
   their lives with this world's
   material possessions
but who arrive empty-
   handed at the door of
   the kingdom of God;
for those whose attitudes
   are always negative
and whose decisions are
   governed by how the
   outcome will affect them.
Lord, in your mercy,
hear our prayer.

May Christ's law of love soften
   hard hearts and transform
   broken lives. **Amen.**

POWER

We pray for those involved
   with power;
for those in government
   or in opposition
and for those who sought
   power and entered politics
because they longed to see
   things change and to
   bring people hope;
for those who have now
   lost their way
and for whom power itself
   has become everything
and for those for whom the vision
   of service still burns brightly.
God of all power,
**we place ourselves in
   your hands.**

We pray for those
   without power;
for those who have nowhere
   to live and who sleep
   on the streets;
for those in poor housing
   or crowded together in
   temporary accommodation;
for those with no voice to
   be heard, no power to
   wield, no place to go;
for those on the margins of life
and for those who are
   made to feel poor
in our materialistic,
   fashion-conscious, status-
   aware generation.
God of all power,
**we place ourselves in
   your hands.**

We pray for those whose
  powers are a burden
and for whom power carries
  an overwhelming sense of
  personal responsibility;
for those who work in the
  National Health Service
and each day are faced with
  decisions of death and life;
for those in the armed forces
who signed up on a wave of
  enthusiasm, or despair,
and are now discovering the
  responsibility laid upon them
to use their powers wisely, with
  compassion and for peace.
God of all power,
**we place ourselves in
  your hands.**

We pray for those whose
  powers are on the wane;
for those who are facing
  a time of illness
and are too afraid even to think
  of what the future may bring;
for those whose minds
  are confused
and who sit all day in their
  chair, seemingly unaware
of the staff, the other residents,
  or family and friends;
for those whose memories are
  all locked up inside them,
having lost the power to
  recall them or share
  them with others.

God of all power,
**we place ourselves in
  your hands.**

In the name of Christ, the
  power of God for us. **Amen.**

FRUIT OF THE SPIRIT: LOVE

Father, we pray for those whose
  love for their neighbours
  takes our breath away;
for those who are prepared to
  risk everything to care for
the sick and the dying, the
  lost and the broken, the
  hungry and the starving;
for those whose love for
  others is a reflection of
  their love for you;
for those whose love for others
  makes them blind to the
  price they must pay.
May the love of Christ
bring them healing and hope.

Father, we pray for those
  who have yet to discover
the depth and the wonder
  of your love for us all;
for those for whom you are just
  a word, or a term of abuse;
for those who pass their days in
  the darkness of fear and dread
and for those who daily
  are crushed by their
  sense of aloneness;

for those who are beginning to
   hear the whisper of your voice
and the sound of your
   love in their lives.
May the love of Christ
bring them healing and hope.

Father, we pray for those
   who have lost everything
and from whom the storms
   and disasters of life
have robbed someone to love
   and someone to love them;
for those filled with anger
   and bitterness
and for whom hope and
   love, peace and joy are
   now things of the past;
for those overwhelmed with
   regret and remorse for
   what has happened,
a disabling uncertainty as
   they face what is to come
and a deep sense of being
   unloved and unwanted today.
May the love of Christ
bring them healing and hope.

Father, we pray for those
   who have been so wrapped
   up in their own needs
that they have been blind to
   the concerns of others;
for those whose attitudes
   and behaviour
have destroyed the love
   that once was there;
for those who have abused
   the love they were offered
and for those who abused
   others and, as their
   excuse, called it love;
for those who want to
   know the joy of a loving
   Christian relationship
but their longing remains
   unfulfilled.
May the love of Christ
bring them healing and hope.

Father, this love is the
   fruit of the Spirit,
not something to be won,
   achieved, or deserved.
Your love conquers all things
and brings healing and
   wholeness to those who are
   touched by your grace.
May the love of Christ
bring them healing and hope.

In the name of Christ, who
   is the perfect reflection
   of the love in our
   Father's heart. **Amen.**

FRUIT OF THE SPIRIT: JOY

I am a patient.
I sit here, waiting for my
   turn to see the doctor.
I am torn apart—I don't
   want to see him, but
   I know I must.

How can you speak of joy
   when I know the news
   that he will give me
will change my whole
   life—for ever?
Yet it would mean so
   much to have joy
and would help me to face
   whatever the future brings.
Pray for me.

silence

I am a journalist.
Whether I write for a newspaper
or you see my face on your
   television screen,
my mind is still so focused on
   bringing you bad news
I have lost my ability
   to see the good.
My journalistic antennae
   twitch uncontrollably
when there is a disaster, a
   vicious crime, or some sordid
   encounter to report.
But joy—you must be joking!
Yet it would make life so
   much more bearable
   if I had some joy.
Pray for me.

silence

I am a married person.
Whether husband or
   wife—I speak for both.
Our life together has
   been joyful—especially
   when we first met.
Life was like one long
   honeymoon, and we thought
   it would never end.
When the children came they
   simply added to our joy
as we watched them
   grow and learn.
But somewhere along the
   way we became just
   too busy transporting
   them—everywhere!
Then there were the demands
   of work, church, and the
   things we wanted to do.
Each took its toll, as we saw
   less and less of each other.
Now the children have gone,
   and so has the joy.
Pray for me.

silence

I am a teenager.
I guess joy isn't a word I
   would normally use.
I am looking to experience
   the moment,
the fury and the fun, pleasure
   and excitement—now!
Yes, I know I'm a worry
   to my parents—
they don't approve of me, or
   my friends, or my lifestyle.

I know they try to listen,
   to care, to understand.
But I feel as if I'm on
   a different planet—
   we just can't
communicate anymore.
I remember the days
   when I was little
and deep down I wish it
   could all be as it was.
Joy, you say?
Perhaps that's what I
   really need, what I am
   looking, searching for.
Pray for me.

silence

Lord, in your mercy,
hear our prayer. Amen.

FRUIT OF THE SPIRIT: PEACE

We pray for those who
   long for peace;
for those whose lives are
   a picture of chaos;
for those whose life and
   lifestyle rob them of
   inner tranquillity;
for those whose every wrong
   choice and selfish decision
closes the door more firmly
   on the peace that could
   have been theirs.
May the grace of God touch
   them with his peace.
Our God answers prayer
and we call on his name.

We pray for those who look
   everywhere to find peace;
for those who fill their lives
   with the things of this world
but will arrive empty-handed
   at the door of eternity;
for those who have lived for
   today and have given no
   thought for tomorrow
and for those whose days
   revolve around themselves
and in satisfying their lust for
   pleasures of the moment.
May the grace of God touch
   them with his peace.
Our God answers prayer
and we call on his name.

We pray for those who work
   for peace between nations;
for diplomats, politicians, and
   delegations seeking justice,
   hope, and peace for all;
for counsellors, social workers,
   and all who seek to bring
   peace in human relationships;
for those whose deep concern
   for the well-being of others
brings a pain and a sorrow,
   an anguish and a despair,
   almost too great to bear.

May the grace of God touch
them with his peace.
Our God answers prayer
and we call on his name.

We pray for those who
have lost peace;
for those whose homes
have been wrecked by
the storms of life
and their lives by the
lies of others;
for those who have lost
everything in [*name
any recent tragedy*];
for those who have no one
left of those who really
mattered to them;
for those whose home, family,
and friends are all gone;
and for those who have
a loneliness that is all
too painfully real
and an aloneness that cannot
be put into words.
May the grace of God touch
them with his peace.
Our God answers prayer
and we call on his name.

We pray for those who are
being robbed of peace;
for those facing times of
illness and uncertainty;
for those who have taken their
health and fitness for granted
and for those with endless
visits to hospital for
treatment still to come;
for those robbed of
peaceful sleep
as their minds are a sea of
turmoil, restlessness,
and despair;
for those who carry a burden
of worry for others
and for those who feel
helpless except to listen,
understand, and care.
May the grace of God touch
them with his peace.
Our God answers prayer
and we call on his name.

We bring all our prayers in
the name of the Prince
of Peace. **Amen.**

FRUIT OF THE SPIRIT: PATIENCE

Think of someone in
need of patience;
someone whose eyes
are so fixed on the
goals they have set
they leave themselves no room
to grow, to live, or to learn.
Lord, may your patient grace
transform all our lives.

silence

Think of someone in
   need of patience;
someone who finds it hard to
   be patient with themselves;
whose failure to be loved
   unconditionally
makes it hard for them to
   know and accept that
   they are accepted.
Lord, may your patient grace
   transform all our lives.

silence

Think of someone in
   need of patience;
someone who finds it hard to
   cope when things go wrong;
whose immediate response
   is to blame others
and to avert all responsibility
   being laid at their door.
Lord, may your patient grace
   transform all our lives.

silence

Think of someone in
   need of patience;
someone who needs to begin
   to take the long view;
who today still sees no answer
   to their prayer of yesterday
and must yet discover the
   timetable of God.
Lord, may your patient grace
   transform all our lives.

silence

We ask our prayers knowing
   God will patiently hear
   and answer them. **Amen.**

FRUIT OF THE SPIRIT: KINDNESS

Lord, we pray for those
   who show kindness;
for those who go the extra mile
   and turn the other cheek;
for those whose kindness
   has changed lives
and helped others to value
   themselves and renew
   their hope in you;
for those whose lives will
   never be the same
because of the kindness
   they have received.
Lord, the source of all kindness,
fill the earth with your love.

Lord, we pray for those who
   have received kindness;
for those who have
   been blessed beyond
   their expectations
and those whose riches have
   outstripped their deserving;
for those who have
   accumulated so many of
   this world's good things
but have no sense of gratitude,
   no desire to show something

of the kindness and generosity
 that has been shown to them.
Lord, the source of all kindness,
fill the earth with your love.

Lord, we pray for those whose
 kindness changed our lives;
for those who were there
 when we needed them
and for those who stood by us
 when others let us down;
for those whose kindness
 brought us to Jesus
and whose whole lifestyle has
 been a reflection of his grace;
for those whose kindness and
 words of witness and truth
pointed us to the source of
 all kindness and love.
Lord, the source of all kindness,
fill the earth with your love.

Lord, we pray for ourselves,
 that we may show
 kindness to others
and that all we say and do
 may be shot through
 with the grace and the
 kindness of Jesus.
We pray that the kindness
 we show to one another
will not be restricted to those
 who offer kindness to us.
We pray that our kindness
 will never be rationed,
 or even controlled,
but it will be the indisputable
 evidence that we are bearing
 the fruit of the Spirit.
Lord, the source of all kindness,
fill the earth with your love.

We bring our prayer in
 the name of Christ,
in the love of God, and
 through the power of the
 Holy Spirit. **Amen.**

FRUIT OF THE SPIRIT: GOODNESS

Lord, you are the source
 of all goodness.
We pray for those through
 whom your goodness flows;
those in whom we most
 clearly experience
a sense of your presence and an
 awareness of your beauty.
May your goodness touch
 and change your world
 and our lives.

silence

Lord, you are the source
 of all goodness.
We pray for those whose
 attitudes and values
so reflect those of your kingdom
that they find themselves
 in direct conflict

with the assumptions
   and expectations of
   their neighbours;
those whose goodness is
   not something for show,
   or carefully rehearsed,
but the fruit of your
   Spirit within.
May your goodness touch
   and change your world
   and our lives.

silence

Lord, you are the source
   of all goodness.
We pray for those whose
   goodness is never seen;
for those whose words of
   compassion are heard by few
   and yet whose deeds of caring
   are experienced by many;
for those whose lives are so
   flooded by the grace of Christ
that his goodness overflows
   through them
to touch friends and family,
   colleagues and neighbours,
   old and young.
May your goodness touch
   and change your world
   and our lives.

silence

Lord, you are the source
   of all goodness.

We pray for ourselves and
   for those that we know;
for those whose goodness
   still touches our lives.
We pray for ourselves, that
   as Christ touches us,
so we may become channels
   of his goodness to others.
May your goodness touch
   and change your world
   and our lives.

silence

Lord, you are the source
   of all goodness.
That is why we bring these
   prayers in your name. **Amen.**

FRUIT OF THE SPIRIT: FAITHFULNESS

Lord of all faithfulness,
we pray for those whose
   faithfulness drives them to
   care for your creation;
for those who warn us
   of the damage we are
   doing to planet earth;
for those who challenge us to
   change our attitude toward
   the world around us
and for those who remind
   us of the responsibilities
   you have laid upon us.
The Lord hears our prayer.
Thanks be to God.

Lord of all faithfulness,
we pray for relationships
   that have been blessed
   by a deep sense of trust
   and faithfulness;
for those who know they can
   take for granted one another's
   love, care, and compassion
and who offer nothing but love
   and faithfulness in return;
for homes where children
   thrive in an atmosphere
   of love without price
and for homes where love and
   faithfulness are at a premium;
but we also pray for
   relationships crucified by
   unfaithful behaviour
and for homes wrecked
   by the bitterness and
   distrust that it brings.
The Lord hears our prayer.
Thanks be to God.

Lord of all faithfulness,
we pray for those who
   faithfully respond to the
   challenges laid upon them;
for those who see the pain,
   hunger, and injustice
   in your world
and are driven to turn their
   words of concern into
   deeds of compassion;
for those who transform their
   despair at the situations
   faced by others
into actions that change
   lives and bring hope
to a confused, despairing,
   and divided world.
The Lord hears our prayer.
Thanks be to God.

Lord of all faithfulness,
we pray for ourselves and the
   challenges and pressures we
   face in our walk with Christ;
when our faithfulness to you
   is put to the ultimate test;
for those times when
   following Christ almost
   makes the journey harder
as we are forced to choose
   between being faithful to
   him and his will for our lives
and allowing the world
   to write our agenda.
The Lord hears our prayer.
Thanks be to God.

We bring our prayers
   in the name of our
   faithful God. **Amen.**

FRUIT OF THE SPIRIT: GENTLENESS

Lord, we hold up before you
those whose gentleness
   comes at enormous
   cost to themselves;
those who, because others
   see them as different,

persistently face abuse,
  intolerance, and rejection;
those who do not fight back
  when they face racial abuse
but gently seek to reach
  out in love, to change
  minds filled with hate,
and to reflect the love that Christ
  showed from his cross.
May our society learn once again
  that God's love is for all.
Lord of all gentleness,
hold us in your will.

Lord, we hold up before you
those whose gentleness has
  touched our lives
and given us hope when
  we most needed it;
those whose names will
  never hit the headlines
and whose loving concern
  is known only to those
  who have received it;
those whose words of peace
  and deeds of kindness
make life worth living and
  each day a new joy.
May we hear again the call to
  become unexpected channels
  of God's endless love.
Lord of all gentleness,
hold us in your will.

Lord, we hold up before you
those who gently care for the
  sick and wait with the dying;
those who gently enrich
  young minds
and open doors of learning
  and discovery to others;
those who gently care
  for the poor and bring
  hope to the starving;
those who gently but
  firmly remind us all
to protect the earth
  and to remember to
  whom it belongs.
Lord of all gentleness,
hold us in your will.

Lord, we hold up before you
those whose gentleness enables
  them to love the unlovable,
to touch the untouchable, and
  to forgive the unforgivable;
those whose gentleness
  breaks hardened hearts
and heals damaged relationships;
those whose gentle gifts
  of understanding
have ended conflicts and
  prevented wars;
those whose gentle skills
  of diplomacy
enable communities, once
  deeply embittered,
to reach out across the
  barriers that divide.
May the love of Christ be the
  source of all our gentleness.
Lord of all gentleness,
hold us in your will.

In the name of Christ,
   whose gentle yet powerful
   love is for all. **Amen.**

FRUIT OF THE SPIRIT: SELF-CONTROL

Think of someone whose
   life is out of control;
someone whose lifestyle
   is causing pain and
   anguish to others
and whose lack of self-control
   is a burden to those
   who care about them.

silence

Think of someone whose life
   is extremely controlled;
someone whose life is lived on
   the tramlines of insecurity
and whose lack of self-
   worth prevents them
   from experiencing
the hope, joy, and freedom that
   life was meant to bring.

silence

Think of someone whose desire
   is always to be in control,
who is never content to allow
   others to express themselves;
someone whose dominant
   personality and
   domineering attitude
restrict the lives of others
   and deprive them
of the opportunity to
   know what their lives
   could have been.

silence

Think of someone whose
   self-control is a rock for
   others to build on
and a haven where peace
   can be found;
someone who tirelessly
   works in the background
   to resolve disputes,
heal relationships, and break
   down barriers that divide.

silence

Think of someone whose
   life is still controlled
by the pain they have
   suffered and the abuse
   they have endured;
someone whose life has been
   controlled by their poverty
and whose hopes and
   expectations have been
   limited by ridicule
and by the lack of praise and
   encouragement from others.

silence

Sovereign Lord, we acknowledge
that nothing is beyond
your ultimate control
and we commit our way,
and the way of all those
for whom we pray,
into your loving care. In the
name of Christ. **Amen.**

TIMES OF STRESS

Father, we pray for people
under stress;
for those facing times of
immense pressure
and for those carrying great
burdens in a rapidly
changing world;
for those being left behind by the
ever-increasing pace of life
and for those who are at the
point of breaking because of
the weight of responsibilities;
for all leaders of nations, of
industry, and of unions
and for those with difficult
decisions to make;
for those seeking to bring
peace and harmony to
a broken world.
This is our prayer.
We ask it in Christ's name.

Father, we pray for all whose
lives are under a cloud;
for those whose lives are
filled with despair
and those who are disillusioned;
for those whose lives are
wrecked by fear, anxiety, or
grief that will not go away
and for those who once were
happy and bright and are
now under a cloud of worry,
concern, and illness;
for those facing a terminal
illness and for those
who care for them;
for those struggling with a life-
long, life-changing condition.
This is our prayer.
We ask it in Christ's name.

We pray for people whose
resolve is buckling under
the pressure of temptation;
for those who are
unemployed or have
been made redundant
and are tempted to feel that
they do not matter anymore;
for those with young families
and for those who are elderly
and are tempted to
withdraw through the
pressure of loneliness;
for those who live away
from home for the first
time in their lives
and are tempted to turn their
backs on values they once
knew and accepted.
This is our prayer.
We ask it in Christ's name.

We pray for ourselves and our
   own walk with Christ.
May what we say and
   how we say it,
may what we do and
   how we do it,
may what we have and
   how we share it,
may our lives and how
   we live them declare
   that Jesus is Lord
and the whole of our lives
   be transformed
into an endless act of worship
   and thanksgiving. **Amen.**
This is our prayer.
We ask it in Christ's name.

THOSE WHO SUFFER

We pray for those who
   suffer because of their
   own foolishness;
for those whose addictions to
   illegal drugs and to alcohol
   are wrecking their lives,
their relationships, and
   the future, and are also
   spoiling the lives of
   those nearest to them;
for those whose selfishness,
   greed, and self-
   centred ambitions
have separated them from
   friends and family.
The Lord hears our prayer.
Thanks be to God.

We pray for those who
   suffer because of their
   experience of grief;
for those who have lost
   someone they love and have
   no one to share it with
and for those whose hearts
   are heavy and aching
and there seems to be no
   one who understands;
for those who are finding it
   hard to cope with their
   sadness and sorrow
and for those overwhelmed
   with their grief and
   their feelings of guilt.
The Lord hears our prayer.
Thanks be to God.

We pray for those who
   suffer because of unjust
   governments and
   oppressive regimes;
for those imprisoned for
   their faith in Christ
and for those who suffer torture,
   house arrest, and harassment
because they dare to challenge
   their political leaders and to
   stand on the side of the poor;
for those imprisoned
   without trial
and for those rejected and hated
   even by family and friends
because of their commitment
   to Christ and their
   obedience to God's will.

The Lord hears our prayer.
Thanks be to God.

We pray for those who
    suffer because of their
    experience of loss;
for those who have lost
    their job and with it
    their sense of purpose
    and pattern each day
and for those who are facing
    financial problems through
    no fault of their own;
for those who have
    been required to take
    early retirement
and feel rejected, inferior,
    and unwanted
and for those who feel
    broken and useless
because they have lost all
    meaning and purpose in life.
The Lord hears our prayer.
Thanks be to God.

In the name of Christ. **Amen.**

MOTHERING SUNDAY

We pray for those homes
    with only one parent;
for those for whom each day
    is a struggle to cope,
who are weighed down
    with responsibilities
and have no one with whom
    these can be shared;
for those who feel trapped—
    imprisoned in parenthood—
for whom the doorway
    to change and hope,
    fulfilment and self-respect
never seems open but is
    constantly slammed
    shut in their face.
May Christ, who brought
    hope to a woman at a well,
help us to reach out to
    those who are alone.
The Lord is our brother
and we call on his name.

We pray for homes under strain,
where every conversation
    is shot through with
    feelings of bitterness
and fashioned in the
    mould of their anger;
for relationships that have
    gone badly wrong
and where separation or divorce
    is seen as the only way ahead;
for those who still long
    to start again
but are uncertain if their fragile
    ability to trust has been
    damaged beyond repair.
May Christ the healer
    reach out to them,
that their homes may be
    filled with the spirit
    of reconciliation.
The Lord is our brother
and we call on his name.

We pray for those
   whose home life
is coloured and stained by
   disappointment and despair;
for those who have longed
   to be parents but have
   found this gift is denied;
for those who find it
   hard to speak of this,
   their deepest need;
for those for whom the
   pain and the hurt, the
   anguish and the anger,
the sense of failure and loss are
   simply too deep to share;
for those who are single and
   are made to feel excluded
by our family-oriented
   society and churches;
for those with tears in their
   hearts for the children
   they have lost.
May Christ the source of
   hope hold them gently
that all may know the arms of
   inclusion around them.
The Lord is our brother
and we call on his name.

We pray for all those for whom
   Mothering Sunday is a day
   of sadness and dread;
for those for whom it is
   a day to avoid, to get
   through, just to cope;
for those around the world who
   have lost home and family,
especially [*name any
   current world needs*];
for those with no happy
   memories of home
as the place where they
   felt safe, wanted, and
   unconditionally loved;
for those who remember
   only the abuse, the
   scorn, or the neglect;
for those still grieving for
   the childhood they have
   lost, or never had;
for those filled with sadness
   and loss for the parent
   who has died.
May Christ the comforter
   touch them in love
that they may experience the love
   and security that never ends.
The Lord is our brother
and we call on his name.

On this Mothering Sunday
   we give thanks
for our place in God's
   family, the church,
that with all its faults and
   mistakes it is still meant to
   be like a mother or father
to lead us on the
   journey of faith.
We pray for those whose
   lives and words and
   deeds led us to Christ
and for those whose gentle,
   clear witness today

still nourishes our faith,
   and gives us courage
   to walk in hope.
May Christ the Lord
   of his church be the
   centre of all things
that as his body, we
   may be a sign of his
   presence everywhere.
The Lord is our brother
and we call on his name.

In the name of him who
   is Lord of the church,
   the family of God,
Jesus Christ the Lord. **Amen.**

EDUCATION SUNDAY

Lord, we pray for all those who
   are involved in education;
for those who teach, are
   school governors,
or are on school councils and
   parent-teacher associations;
for all involved in the running
   of schools, colleges,
   and universities.
May they demonstrate their
   commitment to sharing
   truth and knowledge.
Lord, in your mercy,
hear our prayer.

Lord, we pray for those
   who are being taught;
for children and young
   people at school,
   college, or university.
May learning become a thrilling
   and exciting adventure.
May they learn to use the power
   that knowledge brings
for the care and service of their
   fellow human beings.
Lord, in your mercy,
hear our prayer.

Lord, we pray for an increase in
   opportunities for education
both in this country and,
   especially, in less developed
   nations of the world;
for the work of [*name any place
   of learning*] and all who
   seek to bring knowledge
of health, agriculture, and
   Christ to all the world.
Lord, in your mercy,
hear our prayer.

Lord, we thank you for all the
   ways we can learn about
   living in your world;
for the opportunities to
   know that you, Lord,
are the source of all that
   is good and true;
for giving us a lifetime
   of learning;
for opportunities for
   growth and discovery.

Open our hearts, we pray, and
  our minds and our lives
to the wealth of good
  things we can learn about
  living and about life.
Lord, in your mercy,
hear our prayer.

Lord, we pray for the
  community of the church.
We ask that you will fill your
  church with the power
  of the Holy Spirit,
that, as your people, we
  may grow together
  in love and joy,
and learn from one another
  more of your love, your
  forgiveness, and your peace.
Lord, in your mercy,
hear our prayer.

In the name of Christ,
  the teacher. **Amen.**

PENTECOST

We pray for those who live each
  day as if there is no God
and for those who exist when
  they could be living;
for those who see the world
  but not its creator
and for those who are filled
  with thankfulness for life
but have no Lord to whom
  they can offer it;
for those who spend their
  days with their minds on
  the things of this world
but have given no thought
  to the life yet to come.
May the Holy Spirit open their
  eyes and unlock their hearts.
Come, Holy Spirit,
send us your power.

We pray for those who
  acknowledge God's presence,
who know all about him but
  for whom he is a stranger;
for those for whom God
  is just a word
and for those who are
  genuinely seeking and
  longing to be found;
for those who have met Christ
  but whose faith is weak
and for those who are
  fearful of what trusting
  him might mean.
May the Holy Spirit bring faith,
  hope, and understanding.
Come, Holy Spirit,
send us your power.

We pray for those who
  feel rejected by God
  and their neighbours
and for those who find their
  lives empty and full of
  darkness and despair;
for those who are full
  of dissatisfaction

and have no delight in the love
   or in the friendship of others;
for those who feel lost, alone,
   and defeated by life
and for those whose lives
   are in turmoil.
May the Holy Spirit bring them
   his peace and hope and love.
Come, Holy Spirit,
send us your power.

We pray for ourselves
   and for his church,
that the mighty rushing
   wind of God's presence
and the fiery evidence of
   his cleansing power
will touch and change our
   whole way of living.
We ask that, because of the
   Spirit's coming, nothing will
   ever be the same again.
Come, Holy Spirit,
send us your power.

In the name of Christ and in the
   power of the Spirit. **Amen.**

COPING WITH STRESS

I am a worker under stress.
I have worked in this
   industry for many years.
I have always enjoyed my job
and going to work each
   day was something I
   looked forward to.

But now the job has changed.
When the company
   downsized the workforce
it meant a huge increase
   in my workload.
I now do the work that once
   was done by three of us.
The pressure to succeed is
   enormous and I don't think
   I can cope much longer.
Pray for me.

silence

I am a mother under stress.
I looked forward to having
   a family of my own
and my children are a
   great joy to me.
But they also are the cause
   of much of the stress
   I face each day.
They both are under school
   age, and very lively,
and are always demanding
   more time and energy than
   I feel I have left to give.
My family lives miles away
   and I don't know many
   people where we live.
I am very lonely and beginning
   to forget who I really am.
Pray for me.

silence

I am a person in the National
   Health Service.
Whether I am a consultant
   or a cleaner, a technician
   or serve in a laboratory,
we all feel the pressure when
   something goes wrong.
We regret every mistake.
But we are all human and
   that means every one of
   us makes mistakes.
Unfortunately for us
   and our patients
ours can make the difference
   between life and death.
Perhaps if we felt more
   appreciated and under
   less pressure
the criticisms might be
   easier to bear.
Pray for me.

silence

I am a young person.
Perhaps you think I am
   too young to have
   problems with stress.
But the pressure from my
   peer group is unrelenting.
I am ridiculed because I don't
   want to get involved with
   drink, drugs, or sex.
In a strange way my
   parents' pride
and desire to give me
   encouragement and support
sometimes puts me under
   even greater pressure
   to please them.
I feel so alone, and I have
   no one to talk to.
Pray for me.

silence

I am an old person.
Perhaps you think that people
   of my age don't experience
times of stress—but we do!
Will I be able to cope
   on my own?
How long can I keep my
   independence?
What if I am ill—how
   will I manage?
I once longed for time for
   myself—now I have too
   much time on my own!
I was so used to having family
   and friends around me.
Now I find the silence and the
   emptiness almost unbearable.
Pray for me.

silence

We bring all our prayers in
   the name of him who
   is our peace. **Amen.**

ROOTS

Father, we pray for those
  who have no roots to their
  lives or their living;
for refugees and victims of war;
for the homeless and those who
  feel rejected and unwanted;
for those who have lost the
  roots of family and friends
  in the turmoil of their lives.
We pray, give them hope in
  the strength of your love.
The Lord hears our prayer.
Thanks be to God.

Father, we pray for those
  who are uprooted;
for those traumatised by all they
  have faced and are facing
  in this troubled world;
for those deeply hurt by
  violence, injustice,
  and self-interest;
for those facing misery
  and despair;
for those crushed by the
  pain and sorrow that
  breaks many hearts.
We pray for those who
  feel uprooted from all
  they have cherished.
Give them a new sense
  of belonging in the
  love of Christ.
The Lord hears our prayer.
Thanks be to God.

Father, we pray for those whose
  lives are rooted in pain;
for those who face the
  pain of loneliness, fear,
  and separation;
for those who face the pain
  of body, mind, or spirit.
We pray for anyone we know
  to be facing the pain
of anxiety, depression,
  or bereavement.
We pray especially for those
  whose pain is caused by sin—
their own or someone else's.
May the love and the
  joy of Christ be their
  source of peace.
The Lord hears our prayer.
Thanks be to God.

Father, we pray for ourselves
  and our own roots.
We pray that you will teach
  and enable us to remember
that our faith is rooted in
  what you did and what
  you are doing in history.
We pray, keep us so rooted in
  the power of the Holy Spirit
and our hearts so fixed
  upon Christ that, being
  rooted in him,
we may be rooted in those things
  that count for all eternity.
The Lord hears our prayer.
Thanks be to God.

In the name of Christ, who
came that we might be
rooted in his love. **Amen.**

LIVES THAT ARE FILLED

We pray for those whose
lives are filled with fear
and for those whose lives are
damaged by neglect or abuse;
for those overwhelmed by
their sense of inadequacy
and insecurity
and for those who have lost
their purpose in life and
their reason for living;
for those facing times of
temptation and needing
the strength of Christ.
May the grace of Christ be
sufficient for all their needs.
The Lord hears our prayer.
Thanks be to God.

We pray for those whose
lives are filled with
darkness and emptiness
and for those facing a time
of great frustration and
unanswered questions;
for those overwhelmed by
the pressures of living
and by the demands of
home and work;
for those struggling to cope
with the needs of their family
and those coming to terms
with their singleness.
May the grace of Christ
bring them his peace.
The Lord hears our prayer.
Thanks be to God.

We pray for those coping
with their disabilities
in a community designed
for the fit and the young
and for those still seeking
acceptance and affirmation
in a culture of prejudice
and indifference;
for those excluded by their
colour or their race, by
their age or their gender
and for those whose poverty,
homelessness, and lack
of employment keep
them locked out.
May the grace of Christ
give them hope.
The Lord hears our prayer.
Thanks be to God.

We pray for those who are
sick or in hospital
and for those who will
never recover;
for those who are dying
and for those who
wait with them;
for those who are depressed,
anxious, or afraid

and for those with great
   problems and no one with
   whom they can share them.
May the grace of Christ
   give them strength.
The Lord hears our prayer.
Thanks be to God.

In the name of Christ. **Amen.**

BIBLE SUNDAY

Father, we pray for our
   own nation.
We think sadly of the
   divisions among us—
black and white, rich and
   poor, old and young,
employed and unemployed,
   haves and have nots.
We pray, give us the
   right words to use
that will break down the
   barriers we erect or allow
   to remain between us.
Lord, in your mercy,
hear our prayer.

Father, we pray for young
   people at school or college.
We know that they are
   places of many words,
words that are new and
   words that are familiar,
words that challenge and
   words that confuse,
words that lead young
   minds forward,
and words that might
   lead them astray.
Help young people everywhere
   to value every opportunity
   to learn new things,
discover deeper truth,
   and stand firm against
   all that is wrong.
May the words we use teach
   others the real value of life.
Lord, in your mercy,
hear our prayer.

Father, we pray for our homes.
Forgive us that so often
   they are the places where
   we use angry, bitter, or
   impatient words.
They are the places where
   we show the least care
about the things we say
   and how we say them.
Forgive us if today we have
   said something unkind,
   unloving, or unhelpful.
We pray, help us to use
   words of comfort, love,
   and understanding.
Lord, in your mercy,
hear our prayer.

Father, on this Bible Sunday,
   we thank you for those
   who down the centuries

have made it possible for us
   to have a Bible of our own,
   and in our own language.
We thank you for the light that
   your Word brings to our lives
and for the way that you speak
   the word we need to hear.
Help us as we read the Bible,
that we may know more
   about ourselves, about
   you, about your world
and the way you would
   have us live in it.
Help us by your Holy Spirit not
   simply to read your Word,
but that in reading it we
   may know Jesus, the way,
   the truth, and the life,
and that, in knowing him, we
   may enter into life that is real.
Lord, in your mercy,
hear our prayer.

We ask our prayers in the
   name of him who is the
   Word of life. **Amen.**

THINK OF SOMEONE

Think of someone whose
   confidence is shaken;
whose high hopes have
   been torn to shreds by
   the actions of others
and whose trust in them
   has proved as secure
   as water in a sieve;
someone whose trust has
   been broken and whose
   reliance on others
has been dashed to the ground
   and they are struggling to
   make sense of their lives.
May their confidence in
   Christ give them hope.

Think of someone
   whose confidence has
   been damaged;
who never had any worries
   about their employment
   or ever imagined that their
   job would be ended;
someone who is mourning the
   loss of meaning for each day,
the loss of purpose for their
   life, and the loss of the
   friendship of their colleagues.
May their confidence in
   Christ give them courage.

Think of someone whose
   confidence is being
   crushed out of them;
someone who is hurt and
   damaged by the pressures
   they are facing;
whose home life or work is
   stressful and demanding;
someone who is overwhelmed
   by the responsibility
   of parenthood.
May their confidence in
   Christ give them peace.

Think of someone whose
 confidence is broken;
someone whose whole life is
 in turmoil and confusion;
someone who no longer
 understands how they feel;
someone overwhelmed by their
 anxieties, worries, and fears;
someone who feels lost,
 empty, and broken
and someone facing a
 time of depression and
 needing reassurance;
someone who blames
 themselves for everything
 and feels guilty, rejected,
 and unworthy.
May their confidence in
 Christ heal them and
 hold them still. **Amen.**

DISASTERS

We pray for those for
 whom today is a day of
 darkness and pain;
for those who have
 received bad news
and those for whom the
 bottom has dropped
 out of their world.
May Christ hold them
 gently in his hands.
The Lord hears our prayer.
Thanks be to God.

We pray for those involved in
 [*name any recent tragedy*];
for those injured and maimed,
 those seriously ill in hospital,
and those for whom life will
 never be the same again;
for families and friends of
 those killed or injured;
for the members of the rescue
 services and hospital staff
affected by all they have
 seen and heard.
May Christ hold them
 gently in his hands.
The Lord hears our prayer.
Thanks be to God.

We pray for those facing years
 of hardship and anxiety;
for those who have lost
 everything in flood,
 earthquake, or storm
and for those who have nothing
 left and nowhere to go;
for those who are afraid
 and filled with despair.
May Christ hold them
 gently in his hands.
The Lord hears our prayer.
Thanks be to God.

We pray for ourselves
 and the concerns that
 trouble our own hearts
 and minds and lives;

for all we know we must
    face in the coming
    weeks and months
and for wisdom to know what
    to say and what to do;
for strength to stand firm and
    for faith to trust the one
    who alone is trustworthy.
May Christ hold us
    gently in his hands.
The Lord hears our prayer.
Thanks be to God.

We leave our prayers in the
    gentle hands of Christ
and trust him to reach
    out in love. **Amen.**

HOLOCAUST DAY

We pray for those who lost
    their family and friends
at the hands of those who
    saw only numbers and
    forgot they were people;
for those who are alone with no
    one to share the memory of
    those who were murdered.
Lord, hear our prayer,
that we may not forget.

We pray for those who
    lost everything—
home and possessions, and a
    sense of their own worth;
for those who lost hope,
    peace, and purpose
and for those whose
    bodies were tortured
    and abused through the
    ideology of others.
Lord, hear our prayer,
that we may not forget.

We pray that those who
    suffered will never
    be forgotten;
that those who were
    allowed to die of hunger,
    or were murdered
through the appalling misuse
    of the skills of others and
    their abuse of power,
will always stand as a
    warning to all the nations
    of the world and every
    generation yet to be born.
Lord, hear our prayer,
that we may not forget.

We pray for those who
    survived and feel guilty
    that they did not die;
for those who still bear the
    marks on their bodies,
in their minds, in their lives, of
    all that they experienced—
the memories that time
    does not erase.
Lord, hear our prayer,
that we may not forget.

We pray for those who still
    face our inhumanity today;

for those who still suffer
   hate and rejection,
   exclusion and death—
simply for being different
   and daring to believe
   that in God's eyes
everyone matters to him:
   we are all equal and
   his love is for all.
Lord, hear our prayer,
that we may not forget.

We pray for our world
   and for ourselves.
We have nowhere to hide;
   no excuses will count.
When we face you, Lord,
   what answer will we give
for when we said nothing
   and allowed others
   to pay the price?
We remember in silence
   those who are dying
   even as we pray.
Lord, hear our prayer,
that we may not forget.

silence

In the name of Christ,
   who suffered and died
   for us all. **Amen.**

CHRISTIAN AID

Lord, we cry out for those
   who can cry no longer;
for those who have sat and
   watched and waited
as they have seen their
   children wither and die;
for those who hunger and thirst
   just to live another day
and for those too weak
   even to care.
Lord, hear the cry of those
   who have everything
for those who have nothing.

Lord, we cry out for those
   who cry for food;
for those hungry in a
   world of plenty
and for those who are poor on
   a planet of great riches;
for those who die of starvation
in the midst of those who are
   dying because of their obesity.
Lord, hear the cry of those
   who have everything
for those who have nothing.

Lord, we cry out for those
   whose tears are never heard
and for those who face
   great injustice
because they have no voice in
   the corridors of power;
for those who have allowed
   the millstone of debt
to hang around the
   necks of the poor
and for those who work to see
   the rich nations of the world

open their ears to the
  cry of the poor.
Lord, hear the cry of those
  who have everything
for those who have nothing.

Lord, we cry out for those
  who cry out for others;
for those who refuse to allow
  us to become complacent
and to close our minds to
  the needs of the poor;
for the work and challenge
  of [*name aid agencies*];
for politicians and
  governments,
that they may exchange words
  for deliberate actions
and good intentions for
  justice and love.
Lord, hear the cry of those
  who have everything
for those who have nothing.

Lord, we cry out with anger for
  those too weak even to care;
for little children with swollen
  bellies and fly-infested eyes
and for mothers no longer
  able to feed their babies;
for parents, whose empty faces
  and Auschwitz-like stares,
speak of a holocaust
  still taking place.
Lord, hear the cry of those
  who have everything
for those who have nothing.

Lord, we cry out for those
  who want a chance to
  live before they die;
for those who want to live
  but who would prefer not
  to rely on our charity.
At the beginning of
  Christian Aid Week
we cry out for those who
  will go door to door
and for those who will give;
for those who would
  find it hard to collect
  envelopes door to door
yet who are willing to give
  themselves freely for
  the sake of the poor.
Lord, hear the cry of those
  who have everything
for those who have nothing.

In the name of Christ, who,
  like the poor, had nowhere
  to lay his head. **Amen.**

SOCIAL CONCERN

Father, we pray for the
  world, your world, with
  all its opportunities,
all its resources, and all its
  potential for good.
We remember with
  deep gratitude its
  beauty, its variety,
and the essential goodness it has
  because you are its creator;

for every way that it is
   a reflection of your
   grace and love.
Teach us and all people, we pray,
   to remember the obligations
that you have laid upon us to be
   good stewards of your world.
The Lord hears our prayer.
Thanks be to God.

Father, we pray for our
   society and for our life
   together as one nation.
At this time when all that is
   good and right, true and just,
is being challenged
   and threatened,
we ask for your loving hand
   to be upon us all.
We pray for those in our society
   who are responsible for
   what we see, hear, or read;
for all who lead, guide, or
   are personally responsible
   for young people.
May we remember our
   obligation to the truth
   of your love.
The Lord hears our prayer.
Thanks be to God.

Father, we pray for those who
   have special responsibility for
   people in particular need;
for those who serve in the
   hospice movement
and for doctors and nurses
   and all who serve within the
   National Health Service;
for those who care for people
   who ruin their lives and
   the lives of others
by their abuse of alcohol
   or illegal drugs,
by their addiction to gambling
   or their involvement in
   child abuse or crime.
The Lord hears our prayer.
Thanks be to God.

Father, we pray for the courage
   to challenge injustice
   wherever we find it,
to battle on behalf of those
   who are oppressed,
to carry the burdens of those
   who are weighed down.
Help us, we pray, always to
   remember that it is the
   gospel of Jesus Christ
and the goodness of your
   love that we proclaim,
and that it is by the power
   of the Holy Spirit
that we are called as your
   church to witness
   that Jesus is Lord.
The Lord hears our prayer.
Thanks be to God.

In the name of Christ, who
   calls and sends us. **Amen.**

APATHY

I am a teacher.
For years I have spent
   time in preparation.
I have agonised over my class
   and spent sleepless nights
worrying over their
   problems and fears.
But the endless paperwork, the
   onerous instructions and
   guidelines from on high,
and the lack of support and
   appreciation have squeezed
   all the enthusiasm out of me
and now I don't care anymore.
I am near my breaking point.
Pray for me.

silence

I am a parent.
My family have been my
   life and I have given
   the best years of my life
   to caring for them.
I never looked for
   anything in return.
But when I look at my life
   now, I have nothing left.
Through the years somehow
   I was wrung dry.
I don't seem to be able to value
   myself or my gifts anymore—
I don't even try.
Pray for me.

silence

I am a Christian.
I have attended church for
   years and held every office
and served in every way I could.
I was out every night on
   some committee,
helping in the youth meeting, or
   sharing in the house group.
But now I hardly pray and
   I never read my Bible.
I attend worship less and
   less and I soon shall
   probably stop altogether.
Pray for me.

silence

I am an environmentalist.
I really thought we could
   make a difference.
I thought that, because of our
   stand, things would change.
I was foolish enough to
   expect everyone to see the
   logic of our argument
and we could change the world.
But I was wrong, so
   terribly wrong!
Things today are much worse
   than when we began.
I feel like giving up
   and giving in—
but where will God's
   good earth be then?
Pray for me.

silence

40 PRAYERS FOR INTERCESSIONS

I am me!
Yes, I am still me—though
 sometimes I do wonder!
I am me, with all my
 faults and failing.
I am me, and God's Word
 gives me hope
and tells me that his love
 will never leave me.
Yes, I am me—even when
 the world ignores me
and others simply take
 me for granted.
Yes, I am me—and I need
 to remember me
a little more each day.
Pray for me. Pray for me.

silence

We ask all our prayers in the
 name of him whose love is
 for ever and for all. **Amen.**

THOSE WHO ARE EMPTY

We pray for the hungry
 people in the world;
for those who are imprisoned
 in a cycle of hunger
 and starvation
and for those who have
 been driven from their
 homes by civil war
and are refugees with
 no freedom at all;
for those whose names
 we do not know
but whose faces we have seen
 on our television screens
and whose futile existence
 haunts us still.
May Christ fill empty lives.
Lord, in your mercy,
hear our prayer.

We pray for those in
 our community;
for those who are our
 neighbours and those
 with whom we work
and for those whom we serve
 and those with whom
 we share fellowship;
for those who are imprisoned
 in unemployment
and are locked out of
 many of the things we
 take for granted;
for those in our community
 who are lonely or alone
and for those who are empty
 and long to be filled with joy.
May Christ touch broken lives.
Lord, in your mercy,
hear our prayer.

We pray for those in
 need of healing;
for those who need to
 feel the touch of God's
 grace upon their lives

and for those who have yet to
   acknowledge their need of
   forgiveness and wholeness;
for those whose lives are
   wrecked by addiction,
either their own or that of
   someone for whom they care.
May Christ heal broken lives.
Lord, in your mercy,
hear our prayer.

We pray for those who
   feel imprisoned by their
   bereavement and loss;
for those overwhelmed by the
   changes they are facing
at home, at school, at work,
   or in their own lives;
for those who are finding
   that the journey of life is
   filled with pain, sadness,
   anguish, or despair;
for those who are locked into
   their need to please others no
   matter the cost to themselves.

May Christ transform
   existence into life.
Lord, in your mercy,
hear our prayer.

We pray for ourselves
   and for any for whom
   we are concerned;
for a new sense of the
   privilege of being God's
   sons and daughters
and of the freedom that
   Christ has won for us;
for the presence of the Holy
   Spirit to empower us
to enter into the freedom that
   will bring glory to God
   and joy to ourselves.
May Christ make us truly free.
Lord, in your mercy,
hear our prayer. Amen.

ABOUT THE AUTHOR

David Clowes, born in Ellesmere Port, left school at fifteen following a secondary modern education. In 1965 he committed his life to Christ at Heaton Mersey Methodist and in 1967 he received God's call into the Methodist ministry. He trained at Hartley Victoria College and gained a degree in theology at the University of Manchester.

David served in a number of churches in the northwest of England before retiring in 2010 after thirty-five years in active ministry. His first book, *500 Prayers for All Occasions*, began as a spiritual exercise during a sabbatical. This was followed by *500 More Prayers for All Occasions*. His third book of prayers, *500 Prayers for the Christian Year*, is based on scriptures from the Revised Common Lectionary.

David is married to Angela, and they have two married sons, a foster son, and four grandchildren.